SOUL RECOGNITION

POEMS BY

FLAVIA URSINO COLEMAN
featuring poem by
Susan Sorensen

COPYRIGHT FLAVIA URSINO COLEMAN AND CONTRIBUTORS 2026©

All rights reserved. Apart from fair dealing for the purpose of private study, research, criticism or review permitted under Copyright Act 1968.
No reproduction, copy or transmission of this publication may be made without written permission.

First Published in Australia by USNCOL Pty Ltd,
188 Scenic Highway, Terrigal, NSW 2260 Australia.
www.monkeybusinessthebook.com
www.monkeybusinessthebook.com/beyond-speciesism
colemanpublishing@outlook.com

eBook ISBN: 9780994271693
Paperback ISBN: 9780994271679
Kindle ISBN: 9780994271686

Book design and formatting by: CreativeAS

 A catalogue record for this work is available from the National Library of Australia.

DEDICATION

To all living beings of feather, fur, fin and skin that they be protected from harm and free from fear.
&
And to my beautiful grandchildren Jacob, Oliver, Isabella, Orion and Amahle.

I pray that you will come to live in a world courageous enough to ask the following three questions...

1. Are animals inanimate objects?
2. Do animals value their lives?
3. Do animals deserve their lives?

And through this that we humans come to discover that although each soul arrives on earth dressed in a different coat that in essence we are all the same.

This is
SOUL RECOGNITION.

♡

ACKNOWLEDGEMENTS

To my dear husband Kevin for his loving support, encouragement and tireless hours in helping craft my poetry into this book.

To all those who have opened my eyes and continue to do so through their knowledge and gentle guidance.

To all those who continue to help make this world a better place for all sentient beings. You truly inspire me.

I can only say
THANK YOU

FORWARD

Flavia Ursino Coleman writes with purpose. Her poetry is not only art – it is advocacy. Tirelessly standing up for animal rights, she uses her words to open our eyes and hearts to lives too often ignored. Her work invites us to pause, to listen, and to see the world from the perspective of animals.

In her remarkable collection Soul Recognition, Flavia asks us to consider what justice truly means. Her poems are honest and deeply moving, sometimes challenging, but always compassionate. They remind us that empathy begins with understanding – and that change begins with care.

Flavia's voice is a call for reflection and responsibility. Through her poetry, she encourages us to question assumptions, to feel more deeply, and to act with kindness. This is literature that matters – writing that seeks not only to touch us, but to transform us.

As you turn these pages, allow yourself to be unsettled, inspired, and awakened. Let these words guide you towards a world where respect and compassion extend to all living beings.

Fiona Sainsbury
Vegan Animal Rights Advocate

CONTENTS

Everything We Touch We Affect	1
Childhood Friends	2
Lies	4
A Real Gentleman	5
In Plain Sight	6
The Only Way A Child	7
The Underground	8
Transformed	10
Don't Ask Me To Say Goodbye	11
Sweet Honey Bee	12
Your Best Mate	14
Her Last Breath	16
Dear Pet Shop Customer	18
No Place To Call Home	20
Rain And Lightening	21
Miss Curiosity	22
Individuality Seen	23
Autumn Sun	24
Mighty Ships Of The Desert	26
A Pillow Of Stone	28

I Remember	30
His Life Sold For A Ticket	31
When We Hurt One, We Hurt All	32
Why	33
Your Table's Prized Centrepiece	34
A Donkey's Nightmare	36
Shadow	37
The Sounds Of Animals Screaming	38
Values	39
At Our Mercy	40
Greed	42
Hero	44
I Love Animals	45
Vegan Means Non-Violence	46
Hearts Woven Tightly	47
Shh	48
Meat Your Fate	51
Will It Be Your Child	52
Charity Without Cruelty	54
Most Animals Die Because	55
Sugar-Coated	56
Lockdown	58

Hey Dear Friend	60
Word Privilege	62
Birth Right	64
Delicate Threads	66
Vanish	67
For We Had Lived A Lie	68
Claiming Enlightenment	70
During Drought	71
Slip Away	72
Golden Glue	73
It May Not Be Everyone's Destiny	74
I Cannot Go Along With	75
Could This Be Love	76
Ego	80
We Do Not Gain Anything	82
Other Publications	83
For The Curious	85
Ways To Connect With The Author	86

EVERYTHING WE TOUCH WE AFFECT

EVERYTHING THAT TOUCHES US AFFECTS US

Flavia Ursino Coleman
(That Vegan Poet)

CHILDHOOD FRIENDS

A collage of childhood friends adorns my mind, bitter-sweet memories etched into my soul. Who knows? Perhaps these may be what some refer to as soulmates. What I do know however, is that they have shaped my life through the trajectory of my choices over the years.

My friends didn't have names as such. Our connection in the main was expressed through unspoken affection which transcended the need for words.

Now, here I find myself as an adult all these decades later, utilising words the best way I can in order to make sense of the world that we once knew. To make sense of the world that surrounds me now. To make sense of the world through their eyes.

Whilst their greatest disadvantage was without doubt their lack of vocabulary, this was never going to present as a barrier to me. In fact, as an adult, each of my words is shaped by echoes back to our mutually shared past. They have long gone; their time cut short. I, on the other hand, pray to live long enough to pay tribute, a debt of gratitude, a chance to ask why did I not know better? A chance to say, I am truly sorry.

As a 60s child of migrant parents, I myself had the disadvantage of limited English during my formative years. The night before I started kindergarten I was given one word to memorise: 'toilet'.

Throughout childhood I often felt lonely. An outsider! I'd known a good Catholic, regimented love. A love of right versus wrong and constant correction. I longed for deeper connections. Now this is by no means a slight against my elders, given they did what they thought best, befitting the times and their staunch culture. If anything, this over time has proven itself an advantage.

Drawing more and more inwardly, I moved beyond the reach of a world that might have otherwise broken me by many of its social norms and conditioning. Those who did reach me however, were my pets. Countless of them, introduced into my life over the years. In them I found solace; soul recognition reflected back to me through their eyes. They were my friends. Each had arrived in a different coat; lambs, goats, sheep, pigeons, chickens, bunnies, guinea pigs - an endless list of souls in feather, fur and fin.

Mysteriously, each without warning vanished from my life. The explanation given to me at the end of my school-days remaining a constant. Each had simply run away!

Now, who's for dinner?

LIES

As children we saw them
The sweetness of a mother hen
The joy a playful goat does bring
Forests of melodies as birds sing

Delicate artistry of butterflies
Big brown cow with soulful eyes
The innocence of a baby lamb
Majestic fish that swim in dams

To harm another, we did not relate
Those lies we learnt, served on a plate

A REAL GENTLEMAN

I stand by your side. I'm holding your hand
It seems a hard world. Do you understand?
I know you love animals, you say you do
You won't eat or hurt them, as so few

The day will soon come, you'll open your eyes
With innocent heart, question their lies
They claim to love animals, carved on a plate
Words are not actions, you cannot relate

You're asking questions, they mock in return
Their actions are lies, a hard one to learn
How my heart aches, for you my grandson
I'll rally beside you, until we have won

In time you will grow, a real gentleman
I'll stand by your side, as your proudest Nan

IN PLAIN SIGHT
(The Royal Easter Show)

The bright morning sky
Steals away night
Whilst an eloquent lie
Hides all in plain sight

Kept in the dark
No viewing allowed
In dungeons stark
Until there's a crowd

Paraded far and wide
The ribbons abound
Competing with pride
Grown men on the town

Gawking congested lines barely shifting
Our eyes pleading in helpless surrender
In hesitation our heads barely lifting
As they outbid for the highest contender

Little fingers excitedly poke
Parents with jovial narrative stroll by
The fatted calf an Easter joke
Indifferent to the terror we cry

Beneath blood red sky
Dismembered prior fall of night
Deceit in plain sight, sold as a lie
In the next room - displayed from a height

THE ONLY WAY A CHILD WILL EAT MEAT IS BY DECEPTION KIDS NATURALLY WON'T HURT ANIMALS

Flavia Ursino Coleman
(That Vegan Poet)

THE UNDERGROUND

The underground
Beneath our feet
Tied and bound
Vacant eyes reflect defeat

Society's blood letting
A satanic curse
Guilt deflecting
Excuses rehearsed

Kids reared on cruelty and violence
Of dismembered bodies of innocence
Our animal cousins brutally silenced
Adults sit in denial of consequence

Spared of guilt the human heart
Grown numb and frozen
Colluding its part
The part each has chosen

Yet to a banquet of consequences
We will in time, all sit
As veils lift dissolving pretences
Painfully aware as reality hits

For was it not we
Who chose the violence?
A karmic rebound we will not flee
Our cries for mercy falling to silence

As smell of blood pervades above ground
We shall fall to our feet
Bloodshed, wars and disease abound
Our vacant eyes reflecting defeat

TRANSFORMED

As a child I'd see them often
Their abounding spirits in joyful dance
I ponder if my generation has but forgotten
Their magic moving all into trance

A lifecycle as unique as her colours adorn
Egg to caterpillar in her constructed silk tight
Soon she'll stop munching, time to transform
From devouring leaves with ravenous might

Liquified inside she'll be suspended in time
The Master's creation delighting her dreams
Designed to re-emerge as one of her kind
Coloured artistry, witness to his esteem

She'll dream of the day when she'll flutter by
Revisiting your garden with exquisite grace
A perfectly patterned, free roaming butterfly
In her wake whispers of heavenly trace

As reward she'll kiss your child's tiny hand
And deliver hope to those who have none
Reminding all of the Master's grand plan
Wings through gentle breeze in golden Sun

Perhaps my generation will in time reminisce
Reflecting upon their actions unwise
Recalling their child's hand, that long, lost kiss
Harm, pesticides, habitat loss; dwindling
numbers, with regret realise

DON'T ASK ME TO SAY GOODBYE

Please don't ask me to say goodbye
My heart ain't ready yet
Nor am I ready to understand why
Or turn out the light, and sleep in fret

Instead tonight, you'll purr by my side
Your gentle paws upon my chest
Tonight, you crawl beneath bedcovers and hide
Curled up safely, in blissful rest

Tonight, my blessings I'll once more count
Chuckling at mischiefs of the day
With joyful laughter your antics recount
Whilst with gratitude, I'll quietly lay

Tonight, I'll feel your precious love
And thank the heavenly sky
Tonight, you'll watch from high above
And wipe my teary eyes dry

Just don't ask me to say goodbye
My heart will not allow
For it simply knows not why
We loved so deeply, nor does it know how

Forever in our hearts, Bella

SWEET HONEY BEE

Oh, sweet honey bee
Why do humans steal from thee?
Your hours of distance and toil
With such disregard they spoil
Taking your food to sweeten their own
While creating theirs, you continue to roam

We humans rely on the hard work of honey bees for pollination.
Their existence on our planet ensures ours.
Honey is their food, not ours to take.
One tablespoon of honey, their entire life's work.
Work we readily steal, with callous indifference.

Often exploited by factory farming, they are held as prisoners to satisfy human taste buds.
With so many alternatives on the market such as rice malt syrup, stevia, maple syrup, dried fruit and agave nectar just to name a few, why steal from our humble brethren?

YOUR BEST MATE

I was so small
You seemed so tall

We rolled and tumbled
Your first steps stumbled

You ran in the park
I chased with a bark

I laid on your bed
Hearing nursery rhymes read

Then big school came
With life not the same

I missed my best mate
I'd wait by the gate

Weekends a treat
We'd walk by the beach

Into love you soon tumbled
Unsteady I stumbled

You held hands in the park
I gave my last bark

I laid on your bed
Hearing love poems read

My big day then came
With life not the same

Missing your best mate
Waiting by the rainbow gate

My life was a treat
Remember us always, as you walk by the beach

HER LAST BREATH

From inside her filthy cage
There faded her lonesome yelp
In a fragile body older than its age
The pitiful dog whimpered for help

By her side another stillborn
Her feeble attempts to lick him clean
To bring him back, not ready to mourn
Her cries unheard, his life unseen

She'd once heard rumours of a world beyond
Of lush green grass and blue skies clear
A world for which she could but long
Of kind words spoken and her heart held dear

Still she laboured through pouring rain
Amidst her litter surrounded that night
Her maternal heart continued to strain
Too weak to go on, she too lost her fight

She'd laboured hard with all she had left
Determined to give each precious one life
With her final goodbye, she took her last breath
Her trapped unborn, neither breath nor life

One by one her puppies selected
As if flavours from an ice cream bar
Those less marketable quickly rejected
At the hands of her breeder, they'd not make it that far

DEAR PET SHOP CUSTOMER

Dear pet shop customer, yes you
With your leather shoes and fancy phone
Choosing which of us to take home
Something to amuse, something new

Perhaps a puppy, from a mum left grieving
Litter after litter her babies stolen
Teeth broken, mattered fur, teats swollen
Cries unheard with each one leaving

Perhaps a fluffy kitten, a designer breed
Exciting and fun, litter tray aside
Furniture ruined, tossed outside
Extra chores you'll not need

Perhaps a bird who all day sings
Calling alone to his mirror shinny
Malnourished and bored his metal cage tiny
Wondering the purpose of his feathered wings

Perhaps a fish to brighten a room tone
Socially isolated in a tank way small
Away from Nature's great ocean call
Swimming aimlessly far from home

Perhaps a hermit crab trapped and caught
Powerless to shed for lack of sand
Or sought larger shells for growth demand
Unable to socialise as he ought

Perhaps a snake bred to delight
Selected patterns for human pleasure
Discarded when no longer a treasure
After years confined in a glass tank tight

Or perhaps you will turn and leave this shop
Opening your heart to one now neglected
From a store just like this on impulse selected
Instead with compassion, you'll choose to adopt

NO PLACE TO CALL HOME

Forgotten in a pound
I was finally found
Taken home
No longer alone

Promised to adore
Too soon shown the door
For getting under their feet
My needs they'd not meet

Missing the kids outside
Without shelter to hide
Barking to play the whole day long
Sad and alone, I no longer belong

Yelled to shut up
They've all had enough
I'm no longer their toy
I no longer bring joy

Back in the pound
I pray I'm soon found
With no place to call home
I'll die all alone

RAIN AND LIGHTENING

Rain and lightening
Thunder is frightening

It's icy outside
I want inside

Your lap I desire
By the crackling fire

A purr and a pat
Your loving cat

MISS CURIOSITY

Greeting the light, she lifted her head
Above her sisters from a tightly packed truck
A cloud of white plumage swept the road ahead
Her gentle presence had me awe struck

Something about her curiosity
The rest of her sisters appeared quite broken
Was this the first and last light she'd see
Observing to what she had awoken?

Grimly the truck was slaughter bound
Soon turning, disappearing from sight
As to this day her memory still hounds
Miss Curiosity, lifting her head, to that first light

INDIVIDUALITY SEEN

Dear sweet angel on earth
Sending you peace from high above
I saw your tears, while you my worth
And as I grew wings, I carried your love

Although our encounter brief
From a packed truck passing by
Our eyes met in mutual grief
I felt your compassion, knowing I'd die

My individuality seen by a stranger
I felt connection like never before
Strengthening my resolve for impending danger
So dry your tears, and cry no more

AUTUMN SUN

How does it feel
That autumn Sun?
Does it feel real
On a new day begun?

How does it feel that Sun
To be blessed by its kiss
As your children run
Through seaside mist?

How does it feel awakened by Sun
As it's beams of light playfully dance
Beckoning a smile and moments of fun
Gifting you a day, and that second chance?

You see
For me
There'll be no Sun
On a new day begun
Or a kiss
In the mist
As my children run
Through seaside fun
Or for me a playful dance
Let alone a second chance

My only fate is one
The slaughter man's gun
A brutal end is all I'll feel
Seen as nothing more - than your meal

MIGHTY SHIPS OF THE DESERT

Terrified, she flees another slain herd
Rounded beneath choppers, screams unheard
Forced betrayal by collar tracking device
For their acceptance, each herd pays the price

Transported long ago, from a faraway land
Untold suffering, at the hands of man
Slave labour for rail and road to build
No longer of use, a bloodthirsty kill

Media tells of numbers set to explode
And land unable to tolerate such load
Ordered cull for the sake of all
Ships of the desert, beneath blazing guns fall

So again, she roams in search of protection
Herds grown wiser, she meets with rejection
A lonesome camel fitted with a Judas' collar
Drowning in her blood, for bloodstock dollar

Unlike her chosen sisters, her suffering will end
From artificial insemination, they cannot defend
Sacred maternal bonds, severed at birth
Dairy milking mothers, for all of their worth

Mothers grieving their babies' removal
Farming practices hidden, for your approval
Soap, chocolates, skin care and fun filled rides
Beneath buttered scones, such cruelty lies

Castrated after birth, their sons grown for meat
Used for entertainment, each earning their keep
Void of dignity they'll remain enslaved
Ridden and raced by humans depraved

Pegs driven through their noses so very tender
Mighty ships of the desert, forced to surrender
In groans of agony brought to their knees
Excruciating torture, they cannot flee

Dear friend, believe not what you're told
Justifications by industry through media sold
For each has the right to live free from hurt
Sweet natured beings – mighty ships of the desert

A PILLOW OF STONE

I rested my head on a pillow of stone
My body given to unfamiliar sensations
My first-time labour, I felt all alone
Birth, following forced impregnation

In pens not far, mothers with new-borns
Soon I'd meet my kid stirring inside
That night I laboured well into dawn
Engorged with love, I felt great pride

I'd never imagined such maternal connection
I cleaned and nuzzled hearing him breathe
His baby goat bleats, I felt such protection
A moment of joy, my heart will not leave

Within hours big boots had appeared
This time, I felt more scared than before
For my kid those thundering boots neared
Sadly, not knowing, I'd see him no more

Each trembling baby stolen away
As mothers we gather to see them leave
His fragile bleats, I hear to this day
In dreams at night, I continue to grieve

He was my first born, by no means my last
Forced pregnancies for milk I produce
Every baby remembered from each year passed
A slave to dairy, to which I'm reduced

Rumours have it, my boys were all killed
My daughters eventually all reappearing
Grieving mothers, captive for the milk we yield
Stolen by humans with cold hearts deceiving

My production dropping soon leaving this place
'Humane' slaughter, means nothing, as I face death alone
Room created for another in this space
A first-time mum, to rest her head, on a pillow of stone

I REMEMBER

I remember mum's nuzzle
The warmth of her breath
My instinct to guzzle
Milk from her breast

The caress of her tongue
Her body close to mine
As a new born I clung
Needing her time

Then footsteps like thunder
I'd see her no more
Does she miss me I wonder?
As I face death alone, on this blood-soaked floor

HIS LIFE SOLD FOR A TICKET

The crowds jeering
A defenceless calf runs
Louder the cheering
A weekend of fun

No mum for protection
He flees terrified
Without reflection
Ticket bought with pride

Noose at his throat, a brutal drag
Crowds roaring loud
Big, burly men brag
His life sold for a ticket – are they still proud?

WHEN WE HURT ONE, WE HURT ALL.
WHEN WE STAND FOR ONE,
WE STAND FOR ALL.
WHERE DO YOU STAND?

Flavia Ursino Coleman
(That Vegan Poet)

WHY

Cat snug on the bed
Calf shot in the head

Dog happy to greet
Lamb calved as meat

Wild bird by humans fed
Mother cow, strung by a leg

Dolphins a delight
Kangaroo shot by night

Time to ask why
We choose to comply

YOUR TABLE'S PRIZED CENTREPIECE

You sit so comfortably numb
As you devour with laughter my flesh
Assured I was stunned with a gun
My body sold to you as fresh

My skin in your mouth
Such crackling delight
Thinking not who I was about
Just your feast be carefree and light

Though I'll introduce myself, if only I may
Afterall, I'm your table's prized centrepiece
Stolen abundance upon which you do pray
Thanking the Lord, as you bow in peace

Just as your life, mine was of value to me
Just as you, I had family and mother I adore
Prisoner of a sow's cage, she'd never be free
Forced to give birth, on cold cement floor

Without pain relief and blade my tail docked
Writhing in agony my testis removed
With callous laughter the workers all mocked
My screams for mercy, their hearts unmoved

Their continued pleasure in my mutilation
With pliers they clipped my teeth
Perhaps their easing of workplace frustration
Tossed around bleeding, I cried for mum's teat

My weaker siblings on concrete slammed
Unprofitable to grow and throw on a truck
Those remaining around mother all crammed
Some bled in agony, some unable to suck

Grown with indifference, in faeces and squalor
Rumours had it that mother had died
I had no idea, that the worst was to follow
As for her comfort, I cried and cried

Finally, the right weight for your prize centrepiece
I thrashed in gas as loved ones before
Friends hearing their fate, their terror uneased
Fighting for life, my hooves left behind on gas chamber floor

A DONKEY'S NIGHTMARE

I watch over you as you silently sleep
In your dreams do you still weep?
A donkey's nightmare in dusty fields
Laden with bricks in carts over-filled

Ill fitted harness prodded and beaten
Wounded and blinded you've barely eaten
Body broken and severely infected
Cannot go on, cast aside and rejected

Finally rescued by loving hearts tender
Living your days as a sanctuary surrender
I pray over time, you'll forget how to fear
Sleep sweetly my angel, and feel my heart near

SHADOW

A shadow crossed your eyes
Your soul flickering in disguise
Your authentic self, unable to distinguish
Your tenderness all but extinguished

Animal adrenochrome, your master addiction
Hijacking you with defensive conviction
Bigger than you, destroying compassion
Demanding animal slaughter with relentless passion

Yet still within, your loving heart beats
That place where your ethics and authenticity meets
And on a quiet night beyond the stars and the silence
You can hear your vegan heart beat against animal violence

So, go ahead, release yourself my friend
Time for cruelty and bloodshed to end
Live with compassion and allow in the light
Connect with their beating hearts, beyond the stars and the night

The sounds of Animals screaming on the kill floor is a sound that will haunt me for life. All for a ten-minute taste sensation. What's more, fish cannot scream. I'd imagine it to be like one of those night terrors that paralyses us from screaming

Flavia Ursino Coleman
(That Vegan Poet)

VALUES

We were countered and were numbered
We never countered in those numbers

You never stopped and never heard
Us crying with our herds

Our eyes you would not meet
You only looked at us as meat

You showed us your life values
When you stole the lives we valued

Away from humans we are calmer
Leaving you to face your karma

AT OUR MERCY

6 levels of hardship, bewildered and broken,
3,000 victims with words unspoken.

First time fresh air on innocent faces,
Sentient beings all broken in places.

Searching for hope without understanding,
Those who bear witness barely withstanding.

The pain, the horror, the sadness prevail,
Humans continue the deceitful tale,

Of humane slaughter, which is a lie,
Where humans defend who they buy.

Feathers all ruffled, twisted and bent,
Dreams of freedom all but spent.

As blinking eyes lock on each other,
Sorrow, fear for one another.

The human soul is in decay,
This was the very last day,

Of this young turkey's life,
Who faced death by knife,

Their eyes, their face and innocence,
Taken without any consequence.

Consumer, funder and the buyer,
Protect, defend to be the liar,

That all is good and all is fine,
But all have crossed the evil line,

And sided with the darkest side,
Making normal nationwide,

That exploiting animals is okay,
Ignoring screams and cries away.

Once shown the truth by those who know,
Their tears of shock begin to flow.

They make the change to their mind,
To live with love, for animal kind

Susan Sorensen

GREED

And did greed itself, for a moment not recognise
Itself in the mirror, as it so coldly stared
Reflections of itself through soulless empty eyes
Vocalising sounds instead, pretending to have cared

Greed reduced us to naught, but units of production
Itemised spreadsheets, headed us as livestock
Carefully calculating us as profits and deductions
Our individuality merged, as if we were just one flock

Aggressively greed stacked us as an economic load
Driving smog filled roads towards our grizzly execution
Terrified we huddled as wheels hit dusty road
Thirsty, injured, pregnant, just some of our confusion

Greed glimpsed in the mirror, as wheels spun hard and fast
It's devouring soulless eyes lusting for its gain
Our identity still unseen, we watched you drive on past
You glimpsed us in the mirror, and you'll glimpse us once again

Next time you may notice a simple word change -
'Bloodstock'
You may notice different lettering as you speed on right ahead
Just a simple word, from when you first read
'Livestock'
Perhaps in time, you'll see beyond the soullessness in your mirror, and glimpse our souls instead

HERO

They'll never know their hero

Those who'll never be born
To grieving mothers who mourn

Those who'll never be enslaved
Needing to be saved

Those who'll never know life
Hanging on the edge of a knife

For it's your presence
That creates their absence

Dedicated to Animal activist and friend Andy Faulkner

I LOVE ANIMALS
JUST NOT TO PIECES

Flavia Ursino Coleman
(That Vegan Poet)

VEGAN MEANS
NON-VIOLENCE FOR ALL
BEINGS

NOTHING GOOD EVER
COMES FROM VIOLENCE

Flavia Ursino Coleman
(That Vegan Poet)

HEARTS WOVEN TIGHTLY

We talk, we laugh, we break bread
Not far from our minds, the slain and the dead
Left behind in the wake of the day
Standing united, banners high, wreaths we lay

Our hearts of camaraderie woven so tightly
Smiles chasing away, the grief we feel nightly
Those screams we cannot unhear
Souls terrified, the slaughter they fear

The world for us hard to comprehend
Man's callous indifference, which he'll defend
Can others for a moment, not see
That for breath of life, no soul should plea?

Still here we sit, with chatter and bread we share
With bonds that tie – untold words of despair

SHH

Shh says Big Pharma
Your animals will spread deadly disease
Please save us responds the farmer
With antibiotics and vaccines to put all at ease

Shh says egg, fish, meat 'n dairy corporation
Upon our dollars the world we'll feed
Funding medical research we'll buy education
Institutions beholden for the funds they need

Shh says educator to GP
Instruct your patients what they must eat
A lifetime on meds and never quite free
Swallowing readily as dairy, eggs, fish n meat

Shh says GP to media who'll cover, and lie
We'll fund your shows and ads with persistence
We've the best health scare money can buy
Requesting research dollars for disease resistance

Shh says media to schools
We demand you do not blow our cover
They may be young though nobody's fools
They'll not eat animals once they discover

Shh says schools to each eager kid
Off to pick fruit from the strawberry shed
But not those dark places traditionally hid
Steering you away from animal bloodshed

Shh says slaughter man to butcher removing puss
We'll disguise and marinate so that no one can tell
Let the consumer buy without any fuss
Animals diseased and a lifetime of hell

Shh says butcher to parent buying meat
Just call it pork or veal or roast for the night
For children will not eat any animal they meet
Make it tasty so they'll not put up a fight

Shh says kid to the parent who then lays sick
I'll love you forever as questions lay dormant
Sensing something I cannot quite pick
I just need more time and not all this torment

Shh says parent to his kid sitting alone
From my grave something I want you to see
So many lessons I've taught in our home
But this final one, will set your soul free

Shh says kid as he soon grows
I'll take it upon myself to go undercover
Witnessing suffering in rows upon rows
Animals screaming, he'll then discover

Shh says law maker to activist, threatening Ag-Gag
Caught! I demand you stop where you are
Don't tell me to shh, as on your lies I now gag
For all suffering 'n terror, I'll raise my voice far

MEAT YOUR FATE

Cancer and heart disease on a plate
Meet your fate
The suffering of meat
We are what we eat

Power of health lies in our hands
Opening our hearts, we understand
No better taste than kindness
Leaving behind deception and blindness

WILL IT BE YOUR CHILD OR A DOG?

We live behind gates in basements cold
Knowing only a life of pain, fear, and isolation
Starved, electrically shocked, and set ablaze
Poisoned by chemicals, disinfectants and detergents

My brothers and sisters live horrors untold
As they are restrained for mutilation
How can man do this? I live in a daze
I plead you release us, our anguish is urgent

Without anaesthetic or pain relief given operations
Unable to speak the horrors of their pain
Skulls scalped open, they are put to sleep
Heads violently bashed, they cannot defend

By government grants and co-operation
Science secretly pursuing profit and gain
Public enchanted by their wondrous leaps
Through deceptive greed this torment depends

My brothers and sisters in terror must die
Countless millions a year by many hands in many nations
Forced to smoke, drink petrol 'n be alcoholic
Given tumors, heart disease 'n blindness

My family in underground basements cry
As the deluded conduct research operations
Pillars of society without time to frolic
Revered as demi-Gods for their loving kindness

Seduced to believe in health and beauty
The wonders of an optimum life man seeks
Millions of us each year condemned to abuse
For man's poor choices, we must die

Alcohol, coffee, meat, fizzy drinks fruity
Shopping trollies overloaded with treats
Air too thick to breathe, soil unworthy for use,
Toxic water – as he suffers, he then asks why?

My brothers and sisters wish you no harm
They are rabbits, pigeons, monkeys and mice
Guinea pigs and others who serve you well
They are sheep and goats and even the hog

Beloved pets in a pound should raise your alarm
Before believing your TV - do think twice
For your unquestioned support they do tell
"Will it be, your child or a dog?"

CHARITY WITHOUT CRUELTY

ARE YOU SUPPORTING VIVISECTION?

Flavia Ursino Coleman
(That Vegan Poet)

MOST ANIMALS DIE
BECAUSE HUMANS EAT
THEM

MOST HUMANS DIE
BECAUSE THEY EAT
ANIMALS

Flavia Ursino Coleman
(That Vegan Poet)

SUGAR-COATED

And did you sit alone
Clutching at your phone
Staring down the line
At a dark and empty time?

Did you feel unseen
As we all watched our screen
The depth of your despair
Wondering if we care?

Told to close the door
On all that you'd worked for
You did as you were told
With no one there to hold

No one saw your pride
As it faded from your eyes
With unquestioned giving
You sacrificed your living

To reassure your doubt
A sugar-coated pay out
Flushed down with a drink
So you'd no longer think

Time to dob in a mate
Government did then state
For disease we must all dread
The television said

For he's not friend but foe
If the line he does not toe
Do not shake his hand
Keep your distance, take a stand

Keep in mind those crying
Mourning those now dying
To disease their lives lost
As we tally up the cost

So alone you stare in space
Your life without a trace
Handful of pills, none, sugar-coated
Another death of despair – to remain unquoted

LOCKDOWN

Your life in confine
No way to define
Dying and living, both equal fears
Your pillow stealing your endless tears

We hear you crying into the night
We feel your sadness, we know your plight
Loved ones missed with excruciating pain
Endless lockdown driven insane

For it's only natural to crave affection
In spite of hearing it's for your protection
Yearning deeply for that tender touch
Missing loved ones so very much

That freedom to feel the rain and the Sun
To hold to your heart that cherished one
So you turn on each other, those you need most
Suspicions of neighbours, as deadly host

Loss of freedoms once taken for granted
In rocking motion words desperately chanted
Listening to those in power with trepidation
Believing them true for their reputation

You wonder if in time you'll feel the Sun once more
And the gentle breeze by the edge of the shore
To sing in the rain a heart filled with glee
Escaping restrictions and finally free

Perhaps you'll hear us crying into the night
Reflect on our sadness and remember our plight
Released from lockdown, headed for slaughter
No Sun, nor gentle rain nor breeze by the water

HEY DEAR FRIEND

While you were quivering inside too afraid to see
I marched the streets so that we'd all be free

While you gossiped about my ideas as berserk
I spent decades sifting mountains of research

While you mocked my compassionate lifestyle choices
I stood between you, in defence of the voiceless

Never once did I intend
To hurt or try to pretend

You see I was just

Following my inner core
Hoping a better world for all

Wanting to stand well prepared
To speak up even when scared

For life is not a popularity contest
It's a divine calling to each do our best

To walk tall in spite of our fear
To stop the gossip and to love all dear

To know that mocking only hides doubt
While our beating hearts know, what life's all about

And as my heart dries away those tears
I'll remember you with fondness the rest of my years

Sincerely your friend

WORD PRIVILEGE

I sift for words, how best to relay
While in a world of slumber you peacefully lay
Innocent souls, who word privilege not hold
From my heart to yours their stories be told

How do I tell of the mother dog who mourns
Kidnapped litters from her barren cage forlorn?
Or of the abandoned cat who births down the drain
Her kittens drowning in the pouring rain?

And those heart-wrenching bellows do I translate
Mother cows calling their babies, can you relate?
How can I describe the shivering sheep
Forced to give birth in cold winter deep?

Or of mouths ripped by hooks of brutality
Paralyzed fish unable to scream their reality?
How do I convey sounds of a whip on a horse
Drowned out by cheers of a gambling force?

Or sounds of the mighty camel tortured to run
Pierced by excruciating nose pegs for your fleeting fun?
How do I speak as you crack open that egg
Of the timid chicken who for life could not beg?

Perhaps I'll not find right words to describe it all
Yet I wonder if in time, you'll suddenly recall
Your tiny heart whispering those truths you once heard
Your innocent voice silenced before your first word

BIRTH RIGHT

To which upon he lays proud claim
Man's conscious evolution an unfolding story
As with each chapter, we show up the same
Those who oppose, those who lead to glory

Words written and spoken chapters unfold
Man generously granting many a right
From oppression and suffering untold
While keeping blind to his own blight

The rights of the wee voice, that of the child
To live innocently, young and so carefree
From pale face, discarded and ever so frail
Pathetic lives churned as victims of industry

The rights of the astute, well-spoken female
To discover, to achieve, and to rightfully earn
Free from exploitation and rape by the male
Unopposed by his hand held high and stern

The rights of the one born a Coloured Man
Whipped by his master and slaved to death
Murder of his children and rape of his woman
Helpless to defend to his final breath

The rights of he who is born gay
Set upon by gangs and beaten in parks
From high moral ground an easy pray
For choosing who he loves in the dark

The rights of animals, purpose bred
For fleeting tastes, sole purpose to die
Better off never born, relieved to be dead
Bludgeoned, screaming, not knowing why

As with each chapter, each right granted
Man erects his back staunch and proud
Singing his own praises, smug and enchanted
Claiming his nobility so high and loud

Born intelligent, his wisdom he'll earn
For it was never his to grant each right
For it was he who stole for a later return
For equality of each, is their birth right

DELICATE THREADS

The Earth lets out a sigh
From generations by
Handed down traditions
Unquestioned frail conditions
Stealing from her sleep
Her precious species weep
Interwoven delicate threads
Who rightfully too, Earth tread

VANISH

If we should vanish into the night
Without trace by morning light
Footsteps by the edge of the shore
Washed away forever more
Twilight shall fall into quiet relief
Echoed with but a tinge of grief
And then the Sun shall rise again
Asking if Man had lived in vain

FOR WE HAD LIVED A LIE

We held them all to ransom
We stole away their offspring
Thoughtless of actions and outcome
Of what in time they'd bring

We held a bloody knife at the throat
Of a discarded pregnant cow
And the gentle natured mother goat
And the breastfeeding sow

We tore down homes of the singing bird
And whipped the pure-bred horse to run
Entitled we gunned down wild herds
For we were, the greater one

Drunk on greed we pilfered oceans
Until her sounds ran dry
No fish, or dolphin or whale in motion
Closing our eyes as they slipped by

We drowned our conscience on a plate
Blood oozing from those without defence
With every bite we sealed our fate
We enjoyed our great pretence

We treated Nature as the enemy
We feared her giving Sun
We hid from fresh air flowing free
We'd not seen what we'd become

Thoughtless of future generations
And the world we'd one day leave
We turned against each other's nations
For we The Chosen, we did believe

Then one day there fell a silence
No sweet bird to sing out loud
Many species perished from our violence
Heads hung low, perhaps we were not proud

That was the day that reckoning came
Fearing we'd catch our children's eye
At last we deeply felt great shame
For we had lived a lie

CLAIMING
ENLIGHTENMENT
WHILST JUSTIFYING
EATING AND DRINKING
VIOLENCE.

WHAT'S WITH THAT?

Flavia Ursino Coleman
(That Vegan Poet)

During drought we tried to feed her
During fire we tried to outrun her
During flood we tried to outswim her
During disease we tried to hide from her
Yet not until we realise that we are her, and choose to live in harmony with Nature Will we know peace

Flavia Ursino Coleman
(That Vegan Poet)

SLIP AWAY

The night our memories stole
Whispers of our soul
Our lives moments brief
Awakening from our sleep
From our lives did we not give?
Did we live but not allow to live?
Did we leave a debt to pay?
And did we let life slip away?

GOLDEN GLUE

Our camaraderie as vegans is much the same as the golden glue used to repair broken ceramics. Our vegan hearts are broken on a daily basis. The ceramic golden glue becomes the strongest part, the healing bond that bind us as vegans.
The golden glue is that silent knowing when we look into the eyes of other vegans. And in our mutual strength, we will continue to fight for our animal cousins.

IT MAY NOT BE EVERYONE'S DESTINY TO SAVE ANIMALS, BUT IT'S IN EVERYONE'S POWER, IN FACT, EVERYONE'S RESPONSIBILITY NOT TO HARM THEM.

Flavia Ursino Coleman
(That Vegan Poet)

I cannot go along with exploitation, enslavement, denial of freedom of movement and natural expression, removal of family and friendship groups, mutilation, scientific experimentation and ultimately death. That's all dark, negative karma and evil.

This is what's being incrementally done to humans, many of whom cry 'victim', whilst they, as I once did, perpetrate the same level of torture on innocent defenceless animals.
This is the cycle of violence that we have all been indoctrinated into by the dark forces.

Most humans are addicted to animal adrenochrome of which they do not realise and ultimately share the same fate of disease, fear and torture as those they pay to have tortured.

I truly believe that our ultimate destiny is the Garden of Eden. A place of love and freedom and not this evil track, trace and control. I cannot help but believe if we were to live and eat in accordance to this state of love and peace, disease and despair would not take hold.

Flavia Ursino Coleman (That Vegan Poet)

COULD THIS BE LOVE?

There is no God! I heard you declare
A moment of silence between us fell
For I knew too well, that place of despair
Our witness to animals, their lifetimes of hell

There'd long been talks of darkness and evil
Of humans with hearts as frozen as ice
Their bloodlust as if possessed by some devil
Devouring flesh as if some holy sacrifice

And as we stood, I deeply pondered
What if God indeed does exist?
And what if God is Love, I wondered
And for animals' collective hell, perhaps their only exit?

Could it be so simple that God is Love, and only Love?
Not some prince of darkness commanding brutal sacrifice
Nor some bearded dictator who sits so high above
Demanding those most gentle pay with their lives the ultimate price

For surely Love could not an innocent lamb behead
Or scold alive a defenceless hen
Or create rape racks for baby calves to be forcible bred
Or confine puppies in a puppy mill to a cold, stark and rusty pen

Surely Love cannot demand grinding chainsaw
Dismember a cow strung high
Consciously thrashing as her rushing blood pours
Her unborn kicking inside, her bewildered bulging eyes questioning why

Surely Love cannot condone ocean animals to suffocate
Fighting for their lives on the end of a hook
Their mouths ripping apart gasping their fate
Surely that ain't Love, but rather some spine-chilling story from some ugly horror book

And surely Love cannot, have us all in blind faith be led
To justify that for life itself a pig should desperately thrash
Paralysed in gas then strung up to be bled
Treated with disregard as less than useless trash

For should Love be real, or might I say God
Would we not in reverence before Her in Nature bow?
Would we not join with Her with the same unconditional Love as an adoring, faithful dog?
Would we not see Her, in every soul from fish to bird to cow?

Would Love condemn their souls to hell through callous indifference and violence?
Would Love have us all choose to otherwise pretend?
Or look the other way taking comfort in our silence?
Or do we stand as one to speak of them and for them loudly to clearly defend?

Perhaps, where there is Love, we unify as a sacred whole
And maybe in Love, we glimpse Her in all living presence
Perhaps where there is Love, we know ourselves through each and every soul
Or perhaps where there is Love, we witness God through our authentic essence

So finally, as beside you I stand
A place where hope replaces despair
Not professing to truly know, nor truly understand
But what if God is Love uniting us in our relentless vision of the hope that we both share?

Dedicated to one who truly inspires me
Andy Faulkner, vegan activist and friend

EGO

"I wish to be happy", she pleads
Her ego scorned, "but you still have needs,

Your health is out of order,
Narrow down, don't look any broader"

"I've obeyed your commands,
Meeting all health demands"

"Ah, but your happiness I'll keep from reach
For your friends betray, your trust they breach"

"Again, I've taken heed of your suggestions
I've distanced from others for my heart's protection

Is happiness yet mine, to have and to hold?"
Her ego scorned with even greater fury, "Your happiness I continue to withhold"

"Your net worth measly with those whom you compare",
Head hung low, happiness she did not dare

And as the days kept rolling by
She felt never enough no matter how she'd try

Her life squandered with each passing year
Faded smiles, love evaporated, held hostage too
each and every fear

Then fell a silence by the still of night
By her side, her long-term companion curled up
tight

She noticed his reassured purr so deeply content
For no greater reason than for the life he was lent

To ego, never did he fall
For his was happiness, not to seek or beg at all

So as one continued to purr through the night
The other passed silently, her happiness still out
of sight

We do not gain anything by harming others, especially the defenceless.

Yet, we have so much to gain when we see ourselves reflected in their eyes. We glimpse our souls, that unspoken joy that love and compassion bring. Freedom lights our souls when we live with integrity - this is SOUL RECOGNITION!

Flavia Ursino Coleman
(That Vegan Poet)

OTHER PUBLICATIONS

MONKEY BUSINESS: A STORY OF SOULMATES AND PRIMATES

Written as a romantic/suspense, this gripping story affords the reader insight into the underbelly of biomedical research and cross species contamination.

Explored through the eyes of cub journalist Estelle Goldstein, daughter of pharmaceutical exec Sam Goldstein and granddaughter of psychic, anti-establishment, animal rights activist Esther Harris, this witty 'faction' provides a story beyond the mainstream.

Chosen for presentation in 2016 at the Byron Bay Writer's festival. Monkey Business: A Story of Soulmates and Primates makes for compelling reading that dares to challenge the conventional worldview.

www.monkeybusinessthebook.com
Book by Flavia Ursino and Kevin Coleman

BEYOND SPECIESISM

This book of poem seeks to express the desire of other sentient beings who share our world and to see the world through their eyes. Though they present in different coats, just as we human animals, they too deserve reverence, respect, protection and equality.

www.monkeybusinessthebook.com/beyond-speciesism
Poetry book by Flavia Ursino Coleman & Friends

OTHER RESOURCES FOR THE CURIOUS

WEBSITE:

WatchDominion
www.watchdominion.org

Save Poppy
www.savepoppy.com

Nutrition Facts
www.nutritionfacts.org

Hidden Crimes (1986) - Animals in Laboratories
www.imdb.com/title/tt2582626

YOUTUBE:

Gary Yourofsky
Best speech you will ever hear

NETFLIX:

Cowspiracy: The Sustainable Secret

What the health

WAYS TO CONNECT WITH THE AUTHOR

EMAIL:

colemanpublishing@outlook.com

WEBSITE:

www.thatveganpoet.com

INSTAGRAM:

@that.veganpoet

CONTACT:

www.thatveganpoet.com/contact

www.ingramcontent.com/pod-product-compliance
Lightning Source LLC
Chambersburg PA
CBHW060501080526
44584CB00015B/1514